Deirdre Hines is an award-winning poet and playwright. She lives on the edge of fable with her seven cats and time-travelling father.

As a child she roamed forests and seashores having adventures, which she recorded in her Nature Diaries. Her first book of poetry, *The Language of Coats* was published by New Island Books and was a bestseller. *The Mermelf – A Fable for Our Times* came to her in a dream while holidaying at Gwythian in Cornwall.

For Daddy
&
For all young readers, everywhere in every time.

When I started writing this small story,
You still believed in the Forest of Dream.
Many seasons have passed, since you stood
underneath her branches, and journeyed up
into the stars. Perhaps, conjugations
of Reason made you forget the elf hiding in
yourself. Mermelf dreamed these pages into life
to gift you back the courage to meet in Dream
your hidden elf, and to fly over anomalous seas.

Deirdre Hines

THE MERMELF

A Fable for Our Times

AUSTIN MACAULEY PUBLISHERS™

LONDON • CAMBRIDGE • NEW YORK • SHARJAH

A CIP catalogue record for this title is available from the British Library.

ISBN 9781398469372 (Paperback)
ISBN 9781398469389 (ePub e-book)

www.austinmacauley.com

First Published 2024
Austin Macauley Publishers Ltd®
1 Canada Square
Canary Wharf
London
E14 5AA

To Begin With

Forget everything you think you know or
thought you knew about how to get from
A to B, from one to twenty, or
from start of story to final page.
Begin again in that place your heart knew
as real, before Mind shut out Imagination.
Back when you mistook her rumblings for
Indigestion or Constipation.
Before logicals strapped on spectacles
and your sight went into hiding along
with treasure maps, fairy eggcup silver,
gnome homes in dappled scyamore shade
and all denizens of *Once Upon a Truth*.

You cannot get there by plane, car or boat;
it cannot be seen with Google maps.
It's easier if you're small or
even if you're very, very tall.
All you need to find your way back to where
every story that you forgot calls home
is to listen not just with your ears,
but with the whole of all your brilliant beat.
Lose your logicals. Open the gate
of heart. Journey back on snatch of song,
forgotten rhyme of billowing surf,

spread of starlight on sparkling strand
to the Mermelves in the cove of Merbay.

Where two moons cast their golden slide
right across ripples of turquoise
waters, mermaids ride dolphins over and
under waves that look like rainbows come alive.
All mythical both here and every
other where are drawn to this shore. But
only here do elfin children gather
seaglass from which to whittle aqua flutes.
One song they sing from within those whittlings
is of an elf called Tonnta who one dawn
paddled his way in a sycamore leaf
across three waters to meet with those merl[1]
he'd watched for thirteen full moon nights.

Not knowing that all merl sleep by day,
he sang within his whittling of forests
and blue-green songs that met one mermaid's
wishes. Among her kind, she made sea maps
but believed in places where trees reached
the sky. Her name was Sea Captain Mara.
Rising from beneath those turquoise waters
upended his sycamore leaf, hurtled
him deep below and deeper still as all
elves cannot swim. Mara waited
for him to surface and wondered at how
his face took on the hue of purple
anemone as it plummeted down.

---

[1] Merl: a collection of mermaids

A land monster after all, was what she
thought as she dived after him into the deep.
The leaf sailed off across the horizon
to another island, where a man called
Daniel Defoe would use it for his
tale, but that's a story from an
earlier time. Meanwhile Mara swam with
her rescue up onto the thronging beach
of the Elven tribe and waited the day
it took his wings to dry. That was the day
both worlds changed, when wrapped in birch bark
nets, the Elves carried her to green dappled
pools in the heart of their Eternal Forest.

From the substance the Shell of Hope secretes
into underwater rock art, the merl
weaved waterproof webbings as covers
for Elven wings. And so from opposites
in kind, (but not of Fate), something special
came to be born. And all this because
of the heart meeting of that first couple,
the pairing of Tonnta and Mara—
It is of one offspring of these pairings,
who came from afar to Merbay,
the one called Xiu, who visited awhile,
that is the subject of this small telling,
lifting the veil on a hidden merstory.

What Is a Mermelf?

If by happy chance you were to see
a mermelf looking up at you from deep
within some sea water or shaded nook,
you'd see yourself reflected in eyes
that shift and change colour depending on
time of year or remembered moment
like when they grew their first set of wings
or when their famous fur took on the hue
of the ancient Wisdom Bears of Thyme.
Perhaps their laugh would tickle your funny
bone too, or you'd join them in a dig
(for mermelves are builders of renown,
not just on land but also on sea beds).

Sometimes a mermelf may look, at first, like
a moving rainbow. This is because they
like to decorate their fur with flowers,
shells or borrowed items from Flotsam
or her cousin Jetsam. (It is even
said they once found the maps that drew
the way to El Dorado, Atlantis
Lyonesse, but lost them to an air balloon.)
Stories of them climbing up and into
magpie nests or hunting after dwarven
hordes are true. Mermelves love shiny jingles

perhaps because their hair is Wisdom Bear brown.
Although there are rumours of Wisdom Bears Blue

Until they reach the age of magical
seven-plus or minus two, all mermelves
can understand everything that is or will
or was. Like all and every child that ever
is or will or was, they know Wisdom
for who She truly is behind the masque
of Learn This Off by Heart instead of Live
Life, Ask Why, Follow Paths of Hearts.
To remember those who rathered reasoning,
The Mereum of Colossal Mistakes
has pictures in its archives of schools,
so that history does not repeat
errors made by lies on the Earth plane.

So, what do mermelf children do instead
of Homework, Tests and Timetables? Simple.
To start, they choose the passion of their heart.
For most, it is swimming with the merl,
where they hear deep water lore from leviathan.
For some, it is climbing with the Elves,
where they sing leaf and bud to greenwood.
For few and far between, it is digging
down into the sand or loam or shale
to chart new pathways between the worlds
with maybe Badgerina, Fennec Fox,
River Otter, Daurian pika, Mole,
Ant or favourite mermelf Aunty.

When Is a Mermelf
Not a Mermelf?

For one in a million, adventure calls.
One such is true subject of this telling.
Her name was Xiu. She came to Merbay
astride Fireflier all on her own.
When portals between the worlds began
to close, chaos rose. Each mermelf clan chose
either a hidden life or a free one.
If mermelves do not decorate themselves,
their fur can blend into the earth, but Xiu
was born a brilliant blue. No place to hide
except in lagoon or pool or sea.
At seven, mermelves grow Elven wings or
mermaid tail, but Xiu had neither of either.

And what was more, she was long past seven.
For seven years in all beings is the Age
of Change, of Rebirth, of Transformation.
Except for Xiu. Although Elder Mermelf owned
many, many memories, he could not
find in his treasure trove any mermelf
as blue, as strange, as different as Xiu.
And so he did what Elders do when
met by something they do not understand
or are afraid of: he pretended not

12

to know. He pretended Xiu was the same
as every other mermelf that ever
was or had been or ever would be.

Elder Mermelf thought it best for Merbay
that Xiu grew into her wings or tail
in a quiet grove. And so Xiu was sent
to stay with Nony Mous in Storyhenge.
Of all the places Xiu had ever been
or seen, Storyhenge was quite the strangest.
Each of the *Seven Tales of Childhood*
had come into being here inside stones
that ringed around an earthen hill
Nony Mous had named Librarium of Stars.
All tales that ever were began here too,
thought up beside a roaring driftwood fire
with flames that sparkled like opals.

Like all mermelf children, Xiu knew the rhyme
and song *A little mermelf hides up there.*
Where? There on the star stair, and so was not
surprised when showed his storeyed Storyhouse.
Each room was a type of stair that when tread on
began to read the tale it held within.
And as each stair was carved from nurse logs
fallen in Firstborn Forest, they held
forgotten histories too. But Xiu had
no interest in anything but escape
from all of this ancient. Like every child
that ever had to leave their homeland, Xiu
was angry at this Merbay exile.

Here's one thing Elder Mermelf forgot
to do with Xiu. He forgot to ask what
it was Xiu wanted. And that dear reader
is the biggest booboo of all booboos
for any mermelf child or any child
for that matter. It is that thing adults
begin to forget, even Elder Mermelves.
The theories are many, but in truth one
and only one reason is recorded
in The Origin Tree, and it is this:
'When you think of what you are and what
you used to were, forget not this cone we
planted in your foreheads at your peril.'

Xiu knew or sensed she knew the reason why
Elder Mermelf had sent her far away
from others her own age – Jelly Jealousy.
Envy that his fur had not one bit of blue.
What Elder Mermelf did not know was this:
Xiu's arrival was accidental.
When one door closes another opens,
and so when the portals between the worlds
began to close, another one opened,
and Xiu flew through it on her Fireflier.
No one thought to ask Xiu if it was sheltering
that Xiu sought or something as simple as
a way back through her home's closed door.

And what was more, Xiu was older than Xiu
looked. 'Have you grown all seven rings?'
was all Elder Mermelf asked, and Xiu

had replied as mannerly as Xiu could:
'Xiu has long passed the growth of seven.'
We all believe what we want to believe,
and although Certainty is Doubt's twin,
Doubt has a habit of disappearing
when most needed, unlike her twin sister
Certainty who prefers to remain put.
But Nony Mous had not scribed the Tales
without learning a thing or two about
taking things on face or fur value.

'So tell me, Xiu, what brought you to this place?'
There is nothing quite so tasty to mermelf
tongue as warm chatter beside a fire,
and Xiu loved nothing better than a good
long talk. Nony Mous was nothing if not
a good listener. And time moved slow
in Storyhenge, which is what time must do
if tales are to be told. So all may have
been quite different for Merbay
had not three things happened at once
and at the same exact time, which is not
the same thing as three things happening.
And everything changed because of these.

Three Things

The star maps Nony used to chart natal
forecasts were strewn about the floor.
Nony had never been so happy
since the invention of the eraser
because, as everyone knows, half the fun
in writing lies in rubbing out words
that do not fit, like when your shoes become
too tight and you go to the shoe shop in
order to find the right size. The other
half of the fun is quite the mystery,
and remains unsolved. The Fireflier
Xiu had arrived on had just like Xiu,
Nony learned, come from the star system Cygnus.

There is nothing quite so heart-warming as
homeplace, but nothing quite so endearing
as when someone expresses genuine
interest in the place where you are from.
The first rule of all real conversation
is this. It must take place in place and both
places must be of equal import. It
is and is not like baking in that when
the first rule is kept, everything becomes
as delicious as primrose pottage and
not sour like yesterday's cold porridge.

For place influences us more than we know,
Which is why there are those that would erase it.

Xiu was so used to coming from Cygnus
that she had long since ceased to think of it
as anything special in any shape
or form. When Nony asked her to tell him
where she was from, he expected somewhere
tried and true like Arcadia or The
Enchanted Forests, Lyonesse
or Xanadu. His pipe fell to the floor
at Xiu's words:'Xiu is Cygnian.'
'Cygnian?' was all Nony Mous could say
in reply. 'Does Nony Mous know my home?'
'Nony Mous has often dreamed of Cygnus.'
'Cygnus catches dreamers with our daughters.'

'I do not know this daughter story, Xiu.
Will Xiu gift it me?' smiled Nony Mous.
'Such a telling will bring me home longing,
and my home longing will worsen after
such a telling unless Xiu knows Nony
will assist returning in any way
Nony can.''Xiu has my word on all the
Alphabets of Stone, Tree and Seven Streams,'
was Nony's answer. And as custom held
great sway in that storeyed house, Nony took
out from underneath his patchwork coat
the Pouch of Oath in which a pebble, leaf
and a phial of water were cradled.

'This Pebble of memory holds promises,
and Nony gives his word he will do all
within his power to aid Xiu. This leaf
fell from The First Tree in Firstborn Forest
and is the voice of my solemn oath.
This phial of water remembers the
time, place and face of any oath sworn,
and if Nony were to break his solemn
word, then every time Nony looked in sea,
stream or river, Nony would see this time
and be forever haunted.'Xiu nodded
as the tiny mouse refilled the Pouch
with his pebble, leaf and phial of water.

'Where I am from, we do not swear an oath.
Why do you feel the need to do so? Is
not your word enough?' asked Xiu shyly.
'I cannot remember such a time, but
perhaps when words were young such oath-taking
was not needed. This is how we seal word
in order to bind it to true intent.'
There was a silence then as both took pause
to think on how happenstance can bring two
complete strangers onto the same pathway.
'I think it is something no one in my
homeland would believe. We do not always
speak in words preferring pictures mainly.

Although sometimes we like to watch the shapes
that their sounds make in the air, which changes
colours and sometimes even solid shapes.'

The feather her host always carried then
took on a brilliant hue. It rainbowed in
his hand before completely disappearing.
'Fireflier!' snapped Xiu. 'They is hungry for flight
and wishes to go home.' Nony was known
for being a kind and courteous host,
but that feather performed a special role
in Nony's journey to his path of scribe,
and he didn't want to lose it. Their burp
spat then upon the hearth wet feather down.

Xiu lifted up the sodden mass and blew
three notes upon it. The first was swan gobble,
the next swan drumming, the last cygnet whistle,
and there on the floor, the feather, as it was
although slightly smaller to Nony's eyes.
'Firefliers are easily bored and can cause
much mischief.' Xiu smiled. 'They never mean to
or almost never mean to. They make great friends
but bitter foes...' trailed Xiu wondering where her
host had gone. 'Where did I put those star maps?'
The sound came from high above; Xiu looked up,
and saw Nony hanging by his tail as
he threw unwanted volumes into the air.

Although not young, Nony was as nimble
as any darting fly. It did not take long
to find natal maps he thought he'd lost
and to toss them down onto the floor.
Fireflier Five was beginning to be
more bored than ever in their life before.

Raising their black webbed foot to scratch behind
their massive ears brought a little relief,
but not much. They thought Xiu may have something
tasty to eat hidden in a pocket,
but Xiu was busy spreading out old maps
any fire fledgling would have known were
out of date. They tried then to distract.

They spread their magnificent neck ruffle
and shook from side to side, guaranteed on
Cygnus at least to bring admiring crowds.
No use. Neither Xiu nor Nony passed heed.
They opened up their wings and set all five
ablaze. Even worse. Xiu snapped her fingers
in warning. Unreal. Never had they been
so ignored. They tried to catch forty
winks of shuteye from some unsuspecting
sleeper, but every dream was guarded in
this antique place. No wonder Cygnus held
no record of the dreamers that dreamed this
place only the Night Mares may have known.

'Here on my old natal chart are drawn
all our known planets and the angles
between them and the astrological
houses. This is where they were when Nony
was born. But Nony has never been
able to understand what Stargazer
squiggled here beside these drawings
of a goose or swan or maybe hen.
We call this constellation Cygnus or

Northern Cross. This star in Cygnus we call
Little Cygnus is a double star, and
maybe what this Stargazer means in
this pair of gold and blue two-headed swans.'

The hardest things to see are those that sit
right in front of our noses. Nony raised
up every single of his fifteen whiskers
in shock. If he had looked at Stargazer's
drawing upside down instead of straight,
each eye would have seen as clear as bell.
Xiu shed a small and tiny crystal burp.
It settled on the floor to roll around
until it stopped and grew from within its lace
a replica of Xiu and Fireflier.
'Are you a crystal carver then, dear Xiu?'
'That is what we call tears,' her whisper answer.
'Each tear holds true picture of its wearer.'

Fireflier Five caught a scent of food from
a far off door. No doubt they lived on tale
and sail or book and hook, instead of meal
in this poor fed place. If Xiu wanted all
to believe all Xiu told them so well, but
not quite true. Fireflier Five could not last one
more star shimmer without a bite of grub,
which is why what happened next passed right by
Fireflier's retreating back. Xiu had one
flaw. Xiu trusted everyone she spoke to.
This flaw had brought her by mistaken trust
to Merbay from Little Cygnus, homelonging
Albireo-her heart's name for home.

Had Xiu told Nony the truth about
the how and why of her arrival, Fireflier
may have stayed to listen. Instead the scent
of meadow flowers and buzzing bees brought
him to the best grazing this side of galaxy.
Truth had waited long enough. Truth had had
enough of being yesterday's news.
Nony Mous began every story
with 'Once upon a truth'. Same old,
same old. What future lay in yesterday etc.
Truth was not called Truth for nothing, and so
just as Xiu thought to open up, Nony
upped and went, vamoosed and vanished.

Truth flies, or so says the oldest proverb.
This time Truth took those words at face value,
and hitched a lift upon them with Nony.
Truth travel is not without its dangers,
but Truth wanted to see what would happen
in a time long ago into the future.
Xiu looked around for Fireflier thinking
that perhaps they had swallowed Nony Mous.
No sign. She bit down then on the worry flea
that needed her to worry and worry
in order for that flea to make a nest
of worry fleas. Xiu began to wonder
what was The Who who silenced her story.

There are certain rules that Nature relies
upon. For most of these, Nature needs Truth.
And the tilt of Axis. Without the tilt,
we'd be without season. Spring fever
brings dancing tree elves to Jabuticaba.
Summer tides signals Festival Season.
Autumn bounty brings back the floating markets
to Merbay. Winter storms are where all
the best adventures against the odds appear
for unlikely heroines. When Truth fled,
everything went head over heels. Axis
was furious. To bring Truth back, She would
need Fireflier, Mermelf, Clock, something else…

The giantess named Axis was a tigress
whose paw had held the ball some call the Earth
afloat in a dark and starry pool for half
a day and in a blue and cloudy sky
for the other half. Axis was special
dreamer. Like every cat there ever
was or like every cat that never was,
Axis liked her sleep. In fact, the only
ones who'd ever seen her had met
her in their dreams. Very few remember
their dreams, which is just what Axis wanted
and needed in order to have the peace
to dream up every season into real.

All real geographers know there's far
more to maps of earth then meets the eye.
But that's a story for another…
The roles that both Axis and Truth played
in this cosmic drama were simple parts.
They'd both auditioned back when the world
was young. Axis opened and closed one eye,
flexed out a claw and sent Fireflier up
into the air. The sudden crash upset
a pile of broken objects lying on
Nony's lawn. The shiny stopwatch was
just what Fireflier wanted to finish off
his outfit. And all this racketty-clacketty

brought Xiu out of home longing and right onto
the lawn. Axis yawned and flexed another
crescent-shaped claw. This was just too easy.
The stopwatch had been thrown down
when its tick ceased its tock, but when Truth left,
its wheels and inner cogs began to move.
Tock tick was better than no tick tock at all.
Xiu was drawn to its sound, following
after Fireflier as they ambled back
along the meadow path. Axis had hoped
they'd see the waiting portal cunningly
disguised as Greek architrave and not
ignore an easy means of departure.

There's something soothing about the mane
of Firefliers when combed and untangled.
Each mane exudes a special aroma
particular to each rider chosen
by each Fireflier. Xiu's nose was lost
in zoberry cordial. (A zoberry
is closest in scent to the raspberry,
but no Earth berry can match its flavour.)
Fireflier Five neighed the name of Albireo
as Xiu hopped into his guiding saddle.
They may both be a long, long way from home
as that saying goes, but they still could show
Storyhenge how to really fly a sky.

Meanwhile

The five hundred panicked Firefliers
let loose on Albireo could not find
their leader. Fireflier Five and Xiu had vamoosed.
The Whistler had long noted the restlessness
of spirit in swoop flight after floating
fields of zorn[2]. After many, many light years
forming Fliers from animal and metal,
Whistler had watched his best leave for Earth
to graze upon Fall yellow wheat fields
and feel dreamed of breezes through manes.
Back when Whistler lived below on Earth,
the Old Languages still were spoken,
and fliers were known as Loshadi.

Reports of portals opening up in
the sweltering undergrowths of vine
from which the infamous Albireon
skyboats were woven had reached
Whistler's ears. Few ventured beneath the
Open Wastes of Desert. Fewer still could
stay there long. Its sounds were strange even for
space. Perhaps, this was why Whistler did not

---

[2] zorn-the infamous yellow flower of Albireo, that Firefliers cannot
resist

believe the whisper mill. But when the two
renegades had not returned in time for
The Great Race, Whistler knew whisper was fact.
He summoned his Fireflier twin,
whispered in their ear and set course for Earth.

It Takes a Long Time to Become Young

And even longer to stay that way
unless you can fly faster than bluebots
zigzagging the skies. Earth is old now.
Even older since The Nomenclatures
became our rulers. Like every ruler
ever made, only a certain number
of numbers, twelve to be exact, can fit
into their shaping of the world. I fitted
into a word I saw and heard but could
never bring myself to write, not wanting
to give power to those with neither heart
nor imagination. But if there is
another one like me, this tale is map.

They tell me my name was Anna back then.
I don't remember, but my number is
as clear as day: 25-03 A.
They taught us numbers, but only a few
were taught how to scribe. We were seditious
And everyone knows what happens when we
seditious meet words: 'Anarchy,' they said.
Every word they did not like began with
the letter 'A'. There was Anastasia,
for one. She led a revolt far off in

the Arctic Wastes, and the image of her
once graced every billboard before they tore
them all down. She too had wings. Raven black.

They said she was a myth. They said she was
made up. There was no such thing as humans
who could fly. That was all barbarity.
They said that all such thought and talk was wrong.
They said they'd teach us how to think right.
We were 'Anomaly'. Throwbacks. Rejects.
As out as stereo or radio.
I lived with the others in the Outerskirts.
One day I saw a picture of a dress
from another age. It had skirt after skirt
heaped one upon the other. Each one looked
soft as spider silk. Not like our Outerskirt.
Old barn houses or regulation tent.

Hunger drove each day in that icy waste.
Only the biggest could grab protein drops
by bots immune to harmful contagion.
The protein sacs smelled of newly sprouted
stinkhorns and were marked with smiling skulls.
I ate with the old and the very young
in a small non-genetically made forest
a half-day's walk from our Outerskirt.
There winds scattered sycamore leaves, bounced
off old oak trunks and rested in silver
birch. And there were creatures that flew.
Not mechanical bots but flesh and blood
creatures of feather and curious eye.

We called her Hedge. She taught us to gather
berry, nut, egg and fruit. Better by far
than that mulch in protein sacs; tasty
too. Told us tales of bygone times when our
kind worked in tandem with all growing things.
When what we saw was seen as vision.
When what we were was received as blessing.
Hedge brought us back from the brink, and then
guided us to the air. For each of us
were, like all living things, quite special, as
we came into this world marked by griffin,
the birthmark that allowed them to banish
us. The mark that on each of us was blue.

Hedge named our forgotten forest, Haven.
Hedge told us what we were: 'Only some of
thee will change. Thee dreams come first, before
thee feathers or thee beak. Some of thee will
be a whistler like me. We know the song
of every bird that ever was or
is or will be. We'll call thee back
to birth form, but some will ignore thee call
and stay as bird for always. No one knows
for sure where we come from, but I say it
has to be we fell from the skies for sure.'
Hedge saved as many as she could from cull,
carried us deep into the heartwood for our change.

It took me longer than the others to fly
my first dreams. Unlike the others, I had
no birth family or blood relative

living by my side. I roosted each night
in a nest of my own making on
the top of Museum Ruin, imagined
by seven magpies, or so I insisted.
My dreams were not of fledgling flight nor did
they resemble anything avian.
Instead, I travelled to the stars in boats
I spent hours sketching on torn out pages
from mildewed museum leaflets scattered
in abandon on each empty level.

I fell in love with Dream and how her world
made me feel. On the stars beyond the moon,
the Nomenclature did not exist.
In worlds that did and did not resemble
Earth, I paddled over stardust lakes.
Alongside tumbled gargantuan white
otters, head over heels over tails,
among the whistling swaying star-reeds.
All watched by the sentry heron
in the e-g-lands of the galaxies.
The leaflet of the longboat had Raven
on its prow. Hedge said Vi Queen had Raven
find land by flying up five thousand feet.

Of all the corvids I would have wished
to be, Raven sat on the highest mast.
Hooked beak, diamond tail, fifty-inch wing span,
ruffled throat feathers with at least seven
different calls. Not so much trickster as top
class performer and mimic. Somersaults,

barrel-rolling, flying upside down.
Better than holopics of painted clowns
chasing after shadows, and Tartary
trapezists swinging high and higher in
the circus dome other children sat in.
Better than comedians they hired
to force-feed us laughter as camouflage.

Better by far to scurry quickly off
with my copy of *The Birdspotter's Guide.*
Only four copies had escaped their purges.
Each page was written on in an unknown
hand, except for on her inside cover.
(Call it quirk or whatnot but I always
see a book as a Her or a She or
as being in longing for such a She
as I.) There some hand that tailed each letter
had written: *'For my dearest daring spy,*
Safe flight. Always Yours in Feather and Sky.
October / November the thirty-first / first.'
Then drawings of the mythical griffin.

This book had cost. More than any other
would pay. Three full moons' worth of rations
and boots. Five pairs. Enough to send me back
into the Earth thinner than the thinnest worm.
In this Outerskirt, Barter and Trade controlled
all transactions, even down to the smallest
swap of crab apple jelly for Exit Pass.
So alike in jowl and voice, no one knew
which was which, unless you placed a bottle

of Sundew on the counter. Barter blew
five whole years of profit on a cargo
smuggled in from The Northern Marshes.
Book was my companion in that lonely.

And proof absolute that we were outlaw
as far back as 1803
when this book was printed. Nomenclature
banned books, closed down the Net and libraries.
The printed word was illicit mind food.
All necessary information was Hive.
Or Swarm. Or Colony. Each was
encoded with their role, their genetic
purpose – except for us. We didn't conform.
Their tests could tell them this right from the time
we tumbled into their numbered records.
Hedge said they had lost their fundamentals,
that what we look at changes by that act.

And so we hid as much as we could from
their prying patrollers. There were rumours
of places where it was safe to be us.
Hedge spoke of a safe place called The Haven.
But I didn't believe her. Such stories were
another way of blanking the mind, like when ash
drifted in slumber banks along the edges
of the hovels they made us call Homeland
and lulled us into daydreaming stupor.
When we all knew deep down the only place
where we belonged was in wind thermal rise
or plunge down into loamy earth for worm
or gift of prey to regurgitate for chick.

But my time was running out. The others
cocked beady eyes of suspicion my way.
Long past the age of transition, there were
many who worried that I was a cuckoo
chick – not of their kind, a different different.
Even Hedge began to mumble about snails,
slow worms, slugs and sloths within my earshot.
Without communication beyond bluebots
patrolling skies, there was no way to know.
I turned inward on myself – paid precious
hoarded metals to remove the silicone
implant imprinted with my number, age
and birth date, packed up and went Forest Feral.

I left the day of my sixteenth birthday
By the time I'd be missed, I'd be deep
in the primeval – that part of the wood
they said was radioactive, that part
even Hedge would not venture into, but that
called out to me from its gnarled misshapen.
I did not know then how timely I was.
That day the Nomenclature called a cull.
Everyone below the age of nineteen
was shipped off. All the rest were divided
into even numbers and sent to the four
quarters of the world Nomenclature told us
was flat. Round Worlders were forbidden.

But I did not know that then. All I knew
was wind across my face and a feeling
that began at the tips of my toes and
spread through every fibre of my being.
Like an anti-virus to cage. Freedom.
Wild Horse Spirit is what the ancients said.
I ran towards the future into past.
That first day in the old primeval wood
saw the birth of my actual self.
Away from hovering bluebots and sidelong
glances, I found an old and mossy cave
from which to begin anew. With a well
for water. A place to name at last as home.

I yearned to build a fire. To gaze within
its flickering warmth. The hollow log I found
would serve as sleeping bag. I needed fire
to dry out moss and cook. The aperture
in the cave roof could serve as natural chimney.
But I was fearful in those first few days.
The protein sacs I'd borrowed from Hedge
were tasteless. This wood was a forest like
no other. One tree held fruits round as the sun.
Were they poison or fruit divine? No Hedge
to ask the name of leaf or bud or bee.
The grove of hazel that I found had nuts
as big as hands. Hunger has no caution.

That night I dreamed my true self. I flew
on wings I'd never seen before
over the forest canopy. And just

like when turning over the pages of
my Book and reading what was written there,
so too this flight was similar. Instead
of wondering where I was in the galaxy,
I knew exactly where I was. And what
was more, I knew the name of every
tree, animal and wind. This was the warp
and weft of sap and soil before the wave
of war tore apart all sinews of Earth.
This wood was full of secret holloways.

Holloways that I hoped would lead me to
The Haven. I woke deep in leaf litter
beside a curious green kakapo.
Above, starlight filtered dense foliage
and scattered silver petals onto bright
suns that now I knew were pomegranates.
Where there were kakapo, there were rimu
trees. Maybe she was just as lost as I.
Nuts from my pocket were quickly scoffed,
and she came looking for some more around
my feet. Except my feet were not my feet.
They weren't even proper passerine
but paws that shot out talons after flex.

I arched my back but flicked a tail instead.
What was I? Was this a dream within a dream?
The kakapo cocked up her beady eye.
All kakapo had disappeared before
Nomenclature arrived. Hedge said it was
just as well. They were too kind for what this

world had just become. Thank feather for that.
Lucid dreaming in a different environment?
The kakapo bit down on my tail.
It hurt. I gave a deep and guttural quork.
I jumped up and flexed a pair of golden
shimmering wings. My head swivelled and in
a pool of night dew stared back at Griffin.

Could it be so? How could this be? Griffin?
I was not Raven, Robin or Redstart.
I was Griffin. Impossible but true.
But how? Griffin was my tribe, my totem
and who I was descended from since Time
began. So how could I, a number from
the Outerskirts be source and genesis?
But here I stood in splendid form of both
queen of highest skies and sparsest plain,
as eagle and as lioness. On wings
of golden lustre, I rose up into
the air to catch a thermal current and
ride it high above the forest canopy.

Rapturous and ravenous for all I
had denied myself for too, too long and
revelling in the somersaulting air,
my first flight brought back buried memory.
Griffin was not extinct. Griffin is born
in need, when warp and weft are in danger.
And all of us who bear her mark could be
Griffin. Her tests are difficult and hard.
It is a lonely sky and plain that Griffin

faces, and only she most pliant can
play all of her many roles, carry all
her many baskets. And ripple after
ripple of time has seen Her return.

Griffin has overseen us all since
story of Earth and Sun and Moon and Star
was first whispered in the air by youngster
Grifflets. Any fledgling egg ever hatched
was imagined into birth by Griffin.
Each tide and turn recorded on sound wave
of quork, caw, trill, ratchet, and kyew.
Griffin guards against imbalance in Nature.
I am 25-03 A and I
am anomaly and I am Griffin,
and I am freer and wilder than those
Nomenclature can ever, ever be.

And as I flew higher above that wood
of ancient vine and bark, every plant and
animal and bird I called in griffin syrinx
answered my summoning dawn chorus.
Blackbird, thrush, wren, tit, robin, chaffinch
and redstart swung wild upon the holly
berry and the ivy. Jackdaw, crow and
rook scattered after their startled bluebots.
Transmissions jammed on communications,
and higher than usual incidences of
civil disobedience occurred in
Numbers never known to have shown
such affinity with irrational numbers.

All day I flew – above cloud, through mountain
pass. Returned the path I'd flown. Searching
for sign of others from my tribe. There was
an eerie emptiness in landscape of
valley, plain and crag. All things of aerial
were long ago learned to bring destruction
in their wake. And all resistance hid deep.
I began to tire. In my mind's eye,
Kakapo waited lonely for my touch.
One new moon began to rise above
the jagged mountain pass. I banked
and hung motionless in that calm gloaming,
then griffed to all Griffin that ever were.

Perhaps If contains all the what might haves
and some more after those. Still Nony Mous
enjoyed the slide through whittled hollowed ash,
thinking it nothing more than youngster prank.
However, Nony did not expect
to land on top of a flying griffin.
The how of ever includes quite a lot,
and Nony had read it almost all, but
Griffin was a mythical fable creature,
which put Nony into quite a pickle.
All pickles have contrary natures
and are acquired tastes, although Nony knew
a few who had walked over Cactus Dune.

I immediately thought bot android,
and pitched a dive to throw it off or kill

it with rise into the Frozen Wastes.
I did not expect it to give me grief.
Bot androids were born Nomenclature
and this one must have strayed off range,
which is why I didn't quite believe
I heard what I heard: 'Not so fast, Griffin!'
And which was why I lost my concentration
and plummeted head over tail into
the waiting petals of a Black Bat Tree.
And still the dratted thing clung tightly on.
And worse than all that, I changed form again.

'Phew! I knew it; you no Griffin are!'
'Little bot, you know nothing about me!'
'By my whiskers, I've been Night Mared!'
he replied. The flight had tired me more
than I could believe. I was hungry
and had little need of a broken android bot.
'Everyone knows just who and what bot is,'
I snapped. 'I do not know this bot. This is
Nony Mous you see standing here, and you,
you must be Night Mare!' A tiding of magpies
landed. In their beaks some offerings
for Griffin. A red shiny apple,
a hunk of bread still warm from clay oven.

'Eat then talk!' was all that I could say
between mouthfuls of apple and bread.
The whiskered bot sniffed the air, but ate
a small portion of magpie gifted food.
Sitting on his shoulder was something so

curious, it almost stopped my chew.
A small and oval shaped mirror sat in
perfect posture (if mirrors can be said
to have posture) with its eight legs dangling
upon Feral Boy's shoulder. Of all
the things most hated and most feared by
Nomenclature, Spider Mirror ranked high.
Spider Mirrors were fabled stuff of myth.

'Nony Mous is mouse not bot! And what are
you eyegazing at?' it spoke with pride.
Hedge said that sometimes after shift we
would see things that came from parallel.
Hedge was wrong. 'You are really here then!'
'It would appear that I am somewhere
other than where I was and not where I
should be!' was grumble-mumbled reply.
Had it not been for that mirror…
'I thought you were bot. Where did you get that?'
'What is bot? 'Feral boy, where have you
been hiding, not to know bot? Just then
Mirror showed me an image of a place:

a ring of shining stones that sang out lines
of tales that stirred my buried memory
of swinging in a hammock hung from
mossed branches of The Rock-a-Bye Tree.
Above me moved a galaxy of stars.
I traced out letters with my finger
that spelled 'Merbay'. To my left a house
that was as crooked and as gnarled

as my griffin claw stood a giant
mouse dressed in a leaf suit, the double
of the Feral boy, and behind him
beside a pile of star maps sat a blue blur
who called 'Cygnus Daughter' out to me.

Spider Mirrors reveal your needed Truth
to those who look within. Nomenclature
and their minions have no reflections.
How did Spider Mirror know the birth home
of Griffin? That was forbidden lore.
Griffin guards against imbalance in warp
and weft by imagining into being
that which can heal breach. 'Your name, Feral?'
'Nony Mous of Storyhenge, changeling child!
And they call you? 'Nomenclature gather
names. I looked into his oval eyes
and knew my need had called him here to aid
a return to Haven or Flight to Heal.

'You can call me Griffin, Nony Mous,'
I said. Just then a thunder burst fell
down upon our heads and sent us all
diving deep into the hollowed tree trunk.
'What kind of rain is this?' wondered Nony.
'Nomenclature rain; ashes from their fires.'
I sighed. 'Best hunker down and try not
to breathe too much of it in.' But Nony
was drawing sigils with some chalk onto
rough bark, whispering chants into the air
that brought images of wild rivers

into my mind's eye. The drops I felt
drip down my nose was extinct rain.

I could not remember ever having
sat inside a river of water.
Every cell rejoiced. I tingled
into my Griffin form, as easily
as breathing. Nony hopped onto my
back and we glided glistening
air up into the cloudbank. Stretched out
below were treetops soughing heavily.
And all was green again. A siren pierced
the rain. I sensed a Holloway and dived,
just missing flock of scout bots. 'Now let
it all begin! 'If griffins could smile, I would
have then, but Holloways are hard to fly.

The Flights of Prophecy

All those who sheltered in The Haven
were known as People of the Book.
No one knew for sure when it first was
written. It was housed in the sacred grove
on the Ancient Rock. Behind it grew
a wall of Jade Vine, that sparkled at night.
Blue-green petals shimmered like drops
falling from a waterfall. Around the base
of this black meteorite bloomed one
sandalwood-fragranced youtan poluo.
The youtan poluo only blooms
every three thousand years. This was omen.
Portent of prophecy. Change was coming.

There were fewer and fewer arrivals
since Nomenclature had gathered all
born with a blue birthmark in holdplaces.
Less scouts returned. Those that did bore grim
tidings of burning forests, black lakes, dry pools.
The Guardians of the Grove had no
other choice. Survival meant retreat.
The oldest of the Guardians foresaw
Nomenclature. She had read it in these
lines: *'When one time of burning forests*
presages the dying of our kind,

follow wild flock to find first people…'
Call her Snow, but her secret name was Star.

For three nights past, she'd had troubled
nest sleep. He haunted her still, even
after all these years. He had disappeared
without a word – no message sent, nothing
on which to pin a feather of hope.
Seasons passed. There was bird lore, The Book or
new fledglings to mentor. No one else
replaced him in her heart. Many tried
and failed. Time softens some hard edges,
but then like the jutting limestone crags
surrounding The Haven, they rebirth.
This is when you see if how you've
flown has been The Flight or not.

For three nights Snow had flown back in
time to those early heady mornings,
when they hunted with the Fire Eagles.
Others called him Whistler, but Flame was her
own pet name for him – Flame and Snow.
Together they had fought Nomenclature.
Together they had found The Haven.
Together they had imagined The Book
back to being. Perhaps the portals he
insisted had brought Nomenclature
to Earth had taken him away. Or
perhaps not. And yet, each night she'd
flown alongside him through strange galaxies.

Which was maybe why she was relieved
when the alarm sounded. Three blows upon
the conch shells – signal of breach in defence.
Her Watchers were ever vigilant.
Hummingbirds were faster than any bot
and did not register on radar.
Snow slipped off her feather mantle
and flew on silent wings into Haven.
Like all Owl, she could localise sound.
Below her, nothing moved. All were hiding
until Owl Guardians gave the call to flee.
She banked and flew higher into misted
cloud cover closer to this strange wingbeat.

Whistler knew the song of every bird that ever
was or were or might be. For too long,
he had chased after and been chased
by dreams. The smell of leaf-litter brought
back memories of Snow, her curved moon beak,
their eerie chuhua-aa duet.
Fireflier sighed. Whistler was hard to lead.
Their instinct called for dive and duck, instead
of glide closer and closer to danger.
Flame had followed his head instead
of his heart. Snow tried to shrug him off
and concentrate on locating the source
of this latest Nomenclature trick.

But his face was right in front of her,
with its yellow flamed sun of beak.
Fireflier snorted as Flame drew hard

on the rein and skidded to a full stop.
Snow hovered in a pocket of warm air.
What do you say to that which owns
each chamber of your four-chambered heart?
Flame bowed his head in regret and shame.
Snow touched her beak to his, beckoned him
to follow. Fireflier kept their thoughts
on the shape of the terrain they entered.
It was considered rude to trespass
on love. Firefliers bypassed desire as rule.

Excepting one thing. Certain meadows
can cause the most peaceful of Firefliers
to abandon all decorum, especially
where the Antirrhinum are concerned
Better known as snapdragon, all young
Firefliers see themselves in petals
of these flowers. Better yet are their
seedpods – tiny macabre skulls hang from
tired stems, and to any that eat them
gift special supernatural powers.
Fireflier could not believe his luck.
Stretched out below, acres of snapdragons
nodded their heads in rhythm with the wind.

Snow circled round one huge limestone
rock, tucked in her wings, then dived within.
Impossible to fly through rock. Firefliers
are much too large to enter narrow
gaps. No doubt, she'd lured them into
some hunter's trap. Fireflier sped

away, but Flame was not leaving Snow
again. Just as a Nomenclature ship
lost its bearings in these empty lands
Flame entered the gap in Haven Rock
and Fireflier faced the empty face
that Nomenclature is unless
Black Swan event like this occurs.[3]

That the captain of this ship was a rogue
adventurer was one thing, that I
and my two passengers chose to veer
left of limestone needle at the same
time a Nomenclature ship threw anchor
was another. Collision in air
was rare in those days. Sometimes the bots
malfunctioned. That was the closest we
ever got to what they once called lightning.
Its red tail was nothing like the forked blue
tail or the white comet path of that
dragonbird Hedge told us died in grief.
But Nomenclature ships drove in swarms.

Hedge had taught us best course of action,
if met by patrol or worse, flotilla.
'Use the force of all collision and
propel higher than you have ever
flown before. Judge impact and if
collision will harm your primaries,

---

[3] A Black Swan event describes an event that comes as a surprise
and that has a major effect.

48

then glide back into your human form.
If the worst comes to the worst and all
is lost, wreak havoc on as many
of their ships as you can by flying
through their pulsing plastic skin cover.
Know they will lose direction in all
the confusion. 'I went for collision.

All anchors of Nomenclature ships are
fitted with devices that find the nearest
aperture on which to lock their grey
cloaked mass. The gap in limestone needle was
the nearest aperture. Fireflier was gorging
deep in snapdragon mass covering
those rocks, when he sensed a grey mass approach.
There is nothing quite as strong as a kick
from Fireflier hooves, nothing quite as
dangerous as disturb of Fireflier feed.
Just as I braced for collision, a
spinning anchor locked onto my beak
and pinioned me in grey amorphous.

The ship began to spin in decreasing
circles as I flew in spirals, ever
increasing as I sought counter spin
in order to break free from the anchor.
A vaporous mist rose up as a cone
of whirlwind drew patterns on stone
needles. *Hang on!* I thought, worried my
passengers would slip and fall onto
those jutting needles. Nothing was quite

as precious to that rogue Captain as
his cargo, his promised future pay,
his pride as pirate. He had one flaw:
Curiosity, his cat. His only friend.

By virtue of her curved and arching
tail and stealth of track, Curiosity
had led him to many hidden nests
where Anomaly harboured. Her lips
curled back and her throat evinced a grewl
whenever prey was near. Captain 9
was torn. To escape this vortex,
the anchor had to be unhooked. But
that was not without its consequence.
To fly these skies as pirate without
an anchor meant using tether ropes.
His crew was tiny – only himself,
the cat and three bots salvaged from bot junk.

Despite his desire to please his cat,
the lure of loot was far stronger for 9.
She would have better days to hunt prey.
Leaning forward to press the release switch,
he countered rebellion for the first
time from his beloved cat. A claw scratch
is painful at best, but when given
by genetically modified cat,
it doubles in force. As Captain 9 started
back in a howl of outrageous shock, he
lost control of his controls, his sense
of ordered universe and his temper

as Curiosity sprung onto the deck.

One scent above all others spurred
her stalk, that one that sold for the highest
price in Nomenclature Pleasure Lounges –
Griffin Scent. One bottle would send any
cat into paroxysm, let alone such
a cat as Curiosity, bred specially
in those early labs to bring down
all and any Anomaly. Of all
tingles that had ever tingled down
my leonine spine, this appearance
of a hybrid cat slowed my wing rhythm
into hover and glide. All those that hunt
lower their haunches before attacking.

'We knew this day would come to pass!' said
Snow when the smallest of the Haven Watch
reported on all that had occurred.
Not only did Wren have the beadiest
of eyes, but their small size allowed them slip
between cracks and gaps in limestone
needle or, in this instance, enemy
craft. What Wren found in the hull was just
as The Book foretold. It was time for Haven
to join the fray and aid our stolen kin.
Nony Mous was in his element. One
thing it is to archive all stories
ever told, quite another to live one.

Of all the *Seven Tales of Childhood* that

ringed the earthen hill, Nony Mous loved
best the one entitled *Corvidi*[4].
Instead of looking from the outside
in, he was inside looking out at
one mottled ginger hybrid lower
her haunches on a ship's spinning deck.
He tensed. I have to admit I thought
I had met my match. Griffins may have
fabled strength but what is bred in a lab
is more than every fable and myth
mixed together. And then she rolled
onto her belly and purred like cream.

Behind every mirror lies many more
reflections than the face of the gazer. In
the face of Captain 9, I saw at least
a hundred different masques, all of which
I'd seen be used to blind the owner
to obeying orders. Between
two beings that love one another stretch

---

[4] Corvidi tells the tale of The First Corvid Twins and their path of
flight to find others of their kind. One flies to the dark side of the
moon, where she meets with Feather People who ask her to find a
safe place for them to roost. Corvidi endures many trials, and travels
to many lands, before choosing Earth as place best suited for her
kind. Corvidi retires to a village in Italy, where she is reunited with
her brother, who is a specialist baker. His Rook Cakes are bestsellers
in Faeryland. Before the two siblings cross into the Land on the
Other Side of Tree Shadow, they embark on a legendary journey to
find the location of The Curing Tree. They meet a stonemason who
inscribes their memoirs on a Standing Stone.

chords of light. Between this Captain
and this hybrid cat stretched blue pulsing light.
Perhaps Spider Mirror could stay his hand
poised to press down on the red button
that would release contagion to kill
us all. Just then the hull doors opened,

and out dropped a net of fledgling outcasts
gathered from The Far Wastes. As gravity
is gravity, there was nowhere to go
but down and no guarantee I could
save them all even if I made a plunge.
I needed to fly higher to save its
passengers. Below, an opening was
forming in my swirling vortex. There is
one special property that vortices
reveal and that every child knows as truth:
there are other worlds within each world
we inhabit. For outcasts such as
Anomaly, it is in birds of flight.

For the child who has lost their homeland,
it is glimpsed in dreams or behind a scent
of flowerheads drooping in the rain.
For Captain 9, it lay in promise
of loot and more loot – although there was
something that called out to him when stroking
Curiosity's mane. For Whistler, it had
lain in thinking all worlds farthest away
being brighter. Now that he had seen
Snow again, he knew he'd rediscovered

his own true world. He had left once
from selfish desire. This time he was
leaving for something other than himself,

for rescue of those children held as
hostage by a system so out of sync
with True. Perhaps all would have gone as
The Book foretold. The Flights of Prophecy
had been foretold to herald a
return to harmony of warp
and weft. There were some who disagreed,
especially as there was some missing
text on that page. One thing was sure though.
A pencil sketch of the exact and
accurate image of the Fireflier
grazing on snapdragons was the First Sign.
A ship made of moving metal, the Second.

Return of the fabled Griffin, the Third.
After that the writing fades, but one
image is impossible to decipher.
Only a blue smudge, which the Guardians
presumed to be nothing other than
ink or water blot. Every scholar
searches for that elusive word that
only appears once in a work or once
in an entire language's written
record – the hapex legomenon.
Had the Guardians of Haven heard
of mermelf, they may have known how
to read the cuneiform of smudged blue.

Mermelves do all their writing with blue
elderzemons[5] and water. And every
mermelf has modus domesticus
of revealing their own writing.
Many choose timeworn traditional
of letters appearing as if by
magic, heated by the flame of a firefly.
But others prefer if their readers
have to find the hidden message in
a picture or two. For Xiu, this was
the only way she knew how to write.
Xiu and the author of the prophecy
did not know any other way to write.

---

[5] 'Elderzemons are the fruit from the zemon trees in Merbay'

How to Really Fly a Sky

To really fly a sky requires more
than wing and beak. For the Cygnian
mermelf, each flight is caught beforehand
by her daughters who gather dreamers
in beaks spun from five famous flowers.[6]
Each mermelf is gifted with the traits
of one of these flowers at birthdate.
Xiu's birthdate and the green jade flower
both fell in The Year of the Return.[7]
Xiu and Fireflier were matched when both
had drawn Cygnian herstories
that hung like tapestries of vapour
trail in the Cygnian skies.

---

[6] The Cygnian daughters were the Pollinators of Legend. The five
famous flowers they rescued from extinction by weaving them into
their beaks were in no particular order: The Kadupul flower, famous
for blooming only after midnight and withering away before dawn.
Its white blooms were allied with the infamous Polar Mermelves.
The Green Jade Flower famous for its luminous quality after
pollination by its attendant bats. Firefliers all have bat DNA. Xiu
belongs to this clan. The Violet flower, famous for its songs. The
Ghost Orchid, famous for its ability to change species at will. The
Middlemist Red, famous for its love story.
[7] When the Exodus from Earth began.

Xiu and her Fireflier drew green
jade flowers with looping tendrils as
mermelf after mermelf raised their eyes
up into the sudden canopy
that appeared for all the world and its
grandmother to have sprouted some huge
green woolly bats, whose fur each mermelf
longed to decorate with sparkly shine.
A melfing[8] began to form, and as
Nony Mous was not there to warn against
any such happening, so happened the largest
melfing in The Merstory of Mermelf
once and once only in Storyhenge.

Firefliers are anything if not vain,
and Fireflier Xiu was no exception.
All Firefliers are given adjectives
instead of names at first hatch like
popinjay, lusty-gallant, Narang
or orange, but become known as
Fireflier and their rider or wing number when grown.
Fireflier Xiu thought this archaic way
a relic of all that was wrong with Whistler
and Earth. They thought that every Fireflier
deserved a special name all of their very
own that arrived as suddenly as
any season or their fiery set of wings.

So Fireflier veered off course from lead

---

[8] A group of mermelves.

of Xiu and drew in curlicue one
name after another that blew on
gentle sea breeze gustings, and like every
whisper that came from that fabled island,
there were those who had ears to listen
in or a chronovisor to see with
like the infamous Crook and Cranny.
Times had been lean since Nomenclature.
No longer could they peddle in book
or tale. Gone was the market for rare edition.
All culture was sedition. Newspaper
sensations from the dim and distant past.

Sent to the Outerskirts to monitor
screenings of flickering holographs
designed to divert and amuse foolish
empty minds, Crook and Cranny undertook
spectacles culled from memorised text
to entertain in an airy cave.
It was on a night of forage deep
within its caverns that they found an object
of legend: Pellegrino's Chronovisor.
By then both Crook and Cranny had pledged
allegiance to revolt. Now they could see
into the future, revisit the past,
and even change it for the better good.

On the night Fireflier Xiu wrote all
the five forgotten names of Fireflier
in golden curlicues of flame across
Merbay's sky, neither Crook nor Cranny

could get their chronovisor to start.
They'd planned and plotted to show old footage
from before this Age of Machine, which
Crook believed began with the first factories
but that Cranny believed began when
whaling ships started their brutal slaughter.
But both brothers believed that unless
something changed the way things were, there'd
soon be nothing left of the world they loved.

'It's broken Cranny!' said Crook. 'There's
no end to this. No sooner are we
one foot forward than something sends us two
steps backward. It's time we shut up
shop, retired to somewhere off their radar,
wrote up our memoirs for the future good.'
'Brother dear, the race is not yet won;
we've just got started. Be patient.
Remember what Hedge told us where she
thought their weakness lay. 'Maybe she was
wrong, Cranny. They took her away. How
could something as large as Nomenclature
fear something as invisible as Dream?'

Just then the chronovisor began
to hum, and across its screen, a text
appeared written in golden curlicues:
*'From behind the seventh wave rode our
first herd, with manes whiter than sea foam,
carrying dreams drawn by wings
made of sails and stitched by rivers.*

They settled by our Cygnian seas,
guarded by crystal water-keepers
who protect all water people.
We call their Whistler Leviathan.
Although the rarest of our kind, nothing
is as wise as our WaterFliers.

There are few who have ever seen
our second and most secretive herd.
The Oracles say they came from Earth
on a ship bound for the place Merbay.
The ship was made of every story
of chance encounter with Faery steed.
Less and less fairy steeds were born
in that Age of Railway and Iron.
Some say a herd of Night Mares sent the ship
off course envious of their cousin's
dappled beauty. Others maintain it was
the only way to preserve this fabled
stock. Faery Fliers will only save

the dreaming of those who shelter horses.'
After each curlicue was air-scribed,
a picture was formed from their soundings.
Not every reader saw the same picture
in their mind's eye, as between
each perceiver and what they perceive
lies a distance that is as far from
Earth as Cygnus or as close. It
depends on the depth of the Imagination.
For Crook whose favourite memory

of his sister was her faery lore,
Fireflier Xiu brought back yearning for
traditions of teeth swapped for silver

in chipped eggcups before they took her.
For Cranny, the sound of whales singing
in clicks and bangs and clacks was his childhood
soundtrack. Unlike his twin brother, he
loved the water. His birthplace was their
graveyard. His first act of sedition
was sabotage of their whaling ships.
If Crook had not sent a virus to the bots
investigating his breach of order,
he would have been the next in line
for cull. Cranny was the idealist
to his brother's practical. How
could he have forgotten Nomenclature

needed sperm oil for their bots? What was
this creature flying through the air? What
manner of beasts were its audience
gathered around a circle of stones? Where
had he seen them before? If he
could get access to a library…
But they were almost all gone. The fires
of Nomenclature had seen to that.
But the mermelves, on the other hand, knew
exactly who they were. What they did
not know was origin of the third herd. If
Cygnus caught dreamers with her daughters,
then fliers from this herd guarded them.

What's in a name? Our smallest herd.
This poem that Fireflier Xiu
wrote in curlicue was known
to every mermelf in Merbay and far
beyond. Fireflier stopped his whirling
dervish flight to listen in delight.
From earth to sea to overarching skies
echoed the song each mermelf child was taught;
"When words were young, they called us moldewarp
& we were too small to know. When words
grew up, the thwack of our shovel forepaws
let loose all they thought they'd buried deep.
But like in every good story

Mermelf has a habit of popping up
when you least expect them to appear.
When books were gold, they buried them deep
& we were too small to know. When books
were gone, the thwack of our shovel forepaws
let loose 'The Birdspotter's Guides'
every copy they thought they'd buried.
Only Mermelf know the secrets of the word.
as far back as moldewarp, when words began.
Only Mermelf know the secrets of the world."
The last labour of moles had disappeared
from Merbay along with Nony Mous'
only copy of 'The Birdpsotter's Guide'.

Nony Mous refused to believe the moles
had taken his most precious possession,
and besides, books as all book lovers know
have a habit of straying when you least
expect it and of turning up at just
the right time. Except that Nony Mous had
also disappeared so it was little wonder
that the melfing felt a-tremble or
a-bumble. This was indeed the best
or the worst of tales they'd ever
been brought into. But Fireflier Xiu
knew nothing of Nony's missing book
nor of how these melfing knew the words

Of the Spymaster Whistler's song.
In Fireflier's confusion, Xiu took
hold of the tale of the next, the fourth herd.
Number four is the number of being.
Squares replaced the curlicues in the
cooling air, as a flight of swallows
chased drowsy gnats as the sun began
to set. All of Merbay understood
the power of the fourth dimension.
They were living in it after all,
but just in case they didn't, both Xiu
and Fireflier did something very
rare indeed. They separated to draw

square after interlocking square, all
of which were four dimensional. What
surprised each watching mermelf, whether
floating in the willowy river
or hovering with outstretched wings
over the swaying meadow flowers,
was how Xiu flew – which is to say she
didn't fly that is, but still she moved
through the air as if it was the ground.
Perhaps the correct word was perambulated.
At any rate, gravity did not
appear to pose her any problem.
One mermelf child asked her grandmother,

'Who is she? How come we cannot walk
on air? 'Grandmothers know almost all
there is to know, but there are questions
and there are questions and this was one
of these. 'Shush, they've begun again-
Look!' And sure enough walking across
the now darkened sky was a procession
of all the writing implements ever
known. Behind a silver river swam
a démoiselle or forest fairy.
As she moved numbers fell like petals
into sparkling waters. This Whistler was
known as The Alchemist of Agde.

She who proved Time was an illusion,
that every storyteller knows. Just
then Cranny had an idea. If
you know anything about ideas,
you'd know they float in the air like seeds
until they find a place to root and grow.
This particular Idea was
fed up waiting for the ideal mind
in which to fulfil its destiny.
As a matter of fact, this Idea was
born in 1803
and had been waiting ever since to
put its fail-safe plan into action.

An Idea from 1803

Cranny and Crook had discovered a handle
hidden in the side of the chronovisor.
If turned once, the images revealed
The Year of Their Arrival, or as
Nomenclature called it – Year One.
Neither Cranny nor Crook could enjoy their
favourite breakfasts for weeks after.
And as breakfast is the meal that sets
the note on which the day is sung, suffice
to say that those weeks were all sung off key.
But what if I turned that handle all
of eighteen hundred and three times?
wondered Cranny over and over.

Marvelling at his ingenuity,
he prepared to crank the handle around.
This is where he and the Idea
would have parted company, were it
not for that commonest of fatal
flaws, laziness. Cranny knew he was
much too lazy to crank that handle
around so many times without falling
asleep or giving up. The Idea
breathed two sighs, one of relief and one
of a shortcut onto a dusty and

forgotten shelf of Cranny's mind:
'How Decimals made Big Numbers Small.'

If there was one thing everyone knew
Nomenclature lived and breathed by, it
was the decimal. Cranny could not
remember how to reduce numbers,
and although he knew the book that did,
there was the small problem of retrieval.
The small fortune he had made on its sale
was one thing, its buyer something else.
He had sold it to a Captain 9.
All he remembered about the ship
he flew was its large and gargantuan cat.
'Crook, that cat, what was its name again?'
'What cat? 'The one on Captain 9's ship!'

'Too long ago, Cranny! Why do you ask?'
'I need that book back! We need it back!'
'We do? And why is that? 'To figure out
a way of not having to turn this handle
eighteen hundred and three times, that's why!'
'Why eighteen hundred and three times, brother?'
'Because that's the date on the handle, brother!'
Cranny felt like spitting. Crook spent so much
time making decisions, it was a
true wonder of the world anything got
done. Here he was again, squinting to
get a better look at the dated handle.
'Well, well Cranny! Look what we've found!'

Cranny bent down to look, but could not
see the thing that had Crook dancing on
his tippy toes. 'Spectacles, Cranny!'
Cranny had many excellent virtues,
and one terrible vice – his vanity.
His face had once graced the front covers
of magazines, and although he still
turned heads, the thorn in his side
was his failing eyesight. When Crook bought
him spectacles, Cranny did not speak
to him for a week. 'You read it out, Crook!'
'You'll have to wear them one day, Cranny.
I thought you liked to look disreputable!'

'Disreputable you say! Really?'
'Truly, really! 'Well, if that's the case!'
For the first time in many, many
years, Cranny saw letters in focus.
'For my dearest darling father, Safe Flight.
Always yours in Feather and Sky.
October / November the thirty first / first.'
And then a drawing of Griffin.
'Oh me, oh my! Crook! What have we here?'
'What we have here, Cranny, is priceless!
Absolute proof that what they said was
myth is truth. Anastasia is real!'
'I never for a moment doubted it!'

'Be that as it may, there are thousands
of others that did and indeed still do!
She was not the gone-wrong clone they said

she was. This proves a line of resistance.
This proves she was Anomaly too!
They said she was grown in a lab.
Now we can prove they lied to us all!'
'The only resistance left are a few
wheelers and dealers like you and I,
Crook! Outside of here who really cares?'
'We cannot give up hope. There has to
be a way to beat them. Anomaly,
we may not be, but our sister was.'

They both looked then at the picture on
the sink of a little wren perched on a
fuchsia tree bright with crimson flowers
and sighed. Crook spoke first: 'We owe it to
Annabella, Cranny, to get them back.
You know we do.' Cranny dipped his hands
deeper in the coat that contained many
hidden pockets and pulled out a crumpled
piece of paper. 'I found this in her bedroom
after they all disappeared. Until now
I thought nothing of it. But now I'm
not so sure, and I didn't want to
upset you more than you already were.'

'Tell me what it says!' was all that Crook
could say. *'For my dearest, darling spy,*
Always yours in feather and flight—'
A sudden sound of sirens startled
them both. 'Nothing else, only those same
lines?' asked Crook. 'There is a connection.
If we can crack it, maybe we can
find her, or—''We'll talk about you
hiding things from me after we find her.
We need to talk to someone who can
slip through the time-space continuum.
No matter how cantankerous she
is, we need to visit Lady Truth.'

There Are at Least Seven
Different Types of Truth

The truth was Lady Truth was tiring of
her masquerade. She was learning far away
hills were no greener in this future
than back at home in cosy Merbay.
Few flowers grew here. Fewer trees.
She missed Merbay's three-leaved clover
fields. Lady Luck and her twin brother
Chance had fled aboard the airship named
Hope. Still, she had garnered a growing
group of followers in her purple
awning, that hung on every tumble
of the runes, on every over-turned
painted stone by her bejewelled hand.

No matter how many times she told
them there was nothing to be gained
by knowing what tomorrow would bring,
they could not live in the here and now.
Too well did Truth know how they really
felt, having come to The Outerskirts
because of that self-same helplessness.
'There are at least seven different types
of truth that correspond to all seven
stages of our journeys through life, around

the planets and inside our inner
worlds. Truth changes as it changes us.
Outside in and inside out continually.

Welcome at last, Messieurs Crook and Cranny.
We three have a lot of truths that have
passed their sell-by date to put to rest,
and the truth is I have grown so
very, very weary of this heartless
place. 'Lady Truth, we have a question,'
began Crook. Instead of an answer, she put
a finger to her lips, left her seat
and walked out into the night to sit
beneath a surviving horse chestnut tree.
'You want to know how this all began,
but the real question is, what does it
mean to say that it is true it began

at all. You do not understand me?'
'Lady Truth, we just want to discover
the truth about our sister Annabella,
and Cranny here has a letter she
may have left as a clue.' Cranny offered
her his precious crumpled paper, but
she declined. 'First, I need you both to
swear you will do everything I ask.'
'Of course, of course, we will. Won't we,
Cranny?' 'Well, yes, I guess!' came his brother's
rather more reticent reply. 'In order
that matters are brought to a close, we
need that chronovisor and some clover!'

'Clover?' asked Crook. 'What on earth is that?'
echoed Cranny. 'I never travel
without my clover – it is my luck,'
she insisted. Neither Crook nor Cranny
knew of anywhere that grew clover,
but they could blag as well as anyone.
'Here in the Outerskirt we call it—
We call it—' This from Cranny, quick to
invent, but Lady Truth was having none
of it. 'Don't lie to me, Cranny!
Clover likes running water and grows in
green. I like to travel with a lucky
talisman, but needs must as need is.'

'If truth be told, we neither one of us
have ever heard of clover. So much
of what was common is gone now from
our tongue since the Nomenclature took over,'
sighed Crook as he unlocked the painted door
of 'The Crook and Cranny Curiosity Store'
and ushered her inside. Instead of bright
oil lamps revealing artefacts from
Before (objets d'art like mobile telephones,
a family bike, all sorts of printed matter)
every shelf was tumbled, every artefact
in pieces on the floor, and what was worse,
they could hear a heavy, snuffly snoring.

Neither Crook nor Cranny nor, truth be told,
Lady Truth herself were possessed of that
quality the ancients called cod

that we know now by its more common
variant as courage. They all three
reversed as one back the way they'd come,
tripping over each other and falling
into a Gordian knot on the floor.
Their lack of stealth and silence aroused
from exhausted slumber the visitors
on the upstairs floor. All they could hear
were treads Cranny imagined as new
Nomenclature bot or even dinosaur.

If there was one thing Fireflier Xiu
hated it was disrupted slumber.
The flight of names they had treated Merbay
and the melfing to had exhausted
all their strength. They hung upside down
and fell deep into dream of another
world. Fortunately for our searchers,
Firefliers visit all their dreamed of worlds
and if they're needed there, there they stay
until some resolution occurs.
Xiu had left her Fireflier for a
little foray around this odd and funny
chamber, to figure out where they were now.

Of the melfing they'd left behind,
they took this interruption as an excuse
for a picnic. Lady Truth disentangled
from the knot and stood up in delighted shock.
'Mermelf! Now at last I can get back home.'
Dear reader you must understand that

Xiu had never met a human before
and took instant and immediate fright.
All mermelves expel a sticky net
of sea honey when met with what, for
want of better word, is known as
an enemy. Just as Crook and Cranny
stood up, this net encased the three of them.

Fireflier Xiu sniffed, smelled sea honey,
and lumbered down the stair to gorge
on this rare treat. Lady Truth despaired
and placed one bejewelled finger on
Fireflier Xiu, sent him a message
from her mind, causing him to cease his
slurping, releasing once again our three,
now not so intrepid, searchers for
the now not so attractive simple truth.
'Now what in all of Nomenclature
are you?' asked Crook. 'A relative of
horse no doubt! said Cranny. 'But what
are all of you?' asked a confused Xiu.

Just then the Chronovisor began to hum,
distracting all five of them from humdrum
introductions and that type of conversation.
'This is Captain 9 calling base. This is
Code eighteen hundred and three. I
repeat…Haven is real…Whistler is here.
Send help. This is Captain 9 calling…'
'Whistler!' Both Xiu and Fireflier ran
over to the suddenly sparking

yellow screen of Crook and Cranny's
chronovisor. 'What is the Whistler?'
asked Cranny. Xiu was so caught up in
home longing she answered right away:

'The Whistler was the original,
a Spymaster who when he changed,
changed into a Tasmanian Tiger
like all his tribe, until a different
type of human arrived in the year
1803. Everything
changed after he lost all his family.
His network gathered the last of all
his kind and other different also—
A fading image of Fireflier
and a tiny fluttering wren
in a meadow of snapdragons flickered
on the screen. Two whoops and woohoos

from both Crook and Cranny but Xiu took
a backward step as Lady Truth clapped
some purple ear muffs on what counted
for her ears. (In all her speed to leave
Merbay and live her masqueraded
life, she mistook sheaves of corn for
ears.) 'Of course, Cranny, Annabella
would hide in the place Grandfather took
us hiking in!' 'She's found at last!'
said Crook tossing his hat up into
the air. Fireflier Xiu was anxious
to escape this claustrophobic place.

Besides they sensed something along their spine.

And so did Xiu. It sounded like hate
but looked like jumbled bits of words.
The more Xiu looked at them, it occurred
to her she recognised them as her own
secret fears. 'Don't look, whatever you
are called. That is how they form, from all
our hidden negatives and terrors.'
'And who are they?' she could not help but
ask. 'We call them Nomenclatures, but
there are other names. Here put this on.
We wear them as antidote and shield.'
The amulet that Cranny handed
her was a simple silver locket.

'How does this smell of zoberry cordial?'
'Each locket holds a scent of a happy
memory to its wearer as a shield,'
said Cranny. 'We need to leave right now,'
interrupted Crook. Fireflier coughed
out a stream of blue icy flame, as
Xiu's shadowed jumbled words stood up.
'We cannot leave them to such monstrous.
We'll have to take them with.' Fireflier
sighed, but nodded their feathered forehead.
Neither Crook nor Cranny had ever flown
before, let alone met such strange creatures,
but the truth was their secret wish was flight.

Only at night did this world look wondrous.
As they flew up into the starred velvet
dark of night, the rubbled ruins below
looked peaceful and at ease. Now there was
time for missed introductions. Now they
all five learned of each other's names.
Their once upon a now truths, their once
upon a hoped-for truths, their once
upon their own home worlds truths. Only
Lady Truth was silent. She sat quite close
to Fireflier Xiu's feathered forehead
and drew pictures down from Cygnus
to use as patterns on Merbay's stones.

Every Ending Is a Beginning,
Every Beginning an Ending

If time is an illusion, then also
so is space. The hull doors had just
opened. I needed to fly higher to
rescue that net of fledgling outcasts
gathered from The Far Wastes. I remember
telling Nony Mous and Spider Mirror
to tie their legs around my bristling fur.
I remember the shock of that cat.
I remember the captain no matter
how hard I try not to. I remember
the vortex and the speed at which it formed.
I remember seeing double or what
appeared to be another Fireflier.

After that nothing. Only some fragments
of lines floating in a bee buzzing breeze.
And those lines became a story bend:
'Remember everything you have written
between these pages will one day be read
by someone or something else. Perhaps
a young girl who imagines the Past
lies just ahead; whose map of the world
charts any Future Nomenclatures
as lying far behind. This reader

sees me then, as I really truly
was, as Griffin. Stories blow Idea
into readers. I griffined to save Hope.

They tell me that when I fell, another
Fireflier arrived and caught in their
feathered mane each single fledgling.
The Haven sent their members to net
Captain 9, his ship and his soporific
genetically engineered cat.
But it was the mermelf they call Xiu
who, when she woke me from my sudden
fall, then spoke to me of a journey
across another galaxy where she
and others like her were asked to catch
dreamers for Cygnus' starry daughters.
'to weave our present, past & future from.'

Each night some members of our newly
forged alliance rescues more and more
anomalies from this tired and broken
world. Crook and Cranny are wanted in
almost every world. Fireflier Xiu and
Fireflier gave Flame and Snow away
in a sacred grove. Nony Mous is now
the special friend of that once-feared hybrid
cat. Lady Truth was reunited with
Spider Mirror, and thanks to that tigress,
Axis is hopeful they can open up
an entrance way to dear old Merbay.
But as for me, well that is what Nony

calls a twist at the end of a story.
I spend my days recording Anomaly.
This evening some shoebill storks delivered
news of sightings of Great Auks diving
deep in ocean waters. Of what
new wars Nomenclature will wage, no one
can foretell, but now that you have heard
our tale, I hope you think differently
and consider helping us. Xiu tells me
all Griffins are sought after by every
Cygnian daughter. I can feel their pull.
It won't be long now before I too
embark again on another journey...

Acknowledgements

None of this would have been possible without the eternal love, humour and belief of my beloved late partner: Geoff West-Osborn. Thank you my darling. I know you are waiting for me on the shores of our own secret sea.

All books need beginnings. This book was dreamed into being after swimming Gwythian seas. Thank you, James Alexander Connors, for guiding the way. And for your love and friendship.

If my mother, Gráinne Hines, had not helped me fall in love with reading, I wouldn't be a writer at all. If my father, Dr. John Hines, had not taught me the lore of the wild, I would not have known how to read Nature's maps. If my brother, Jay Hines, hadn't begged me to make up bedtime stories, I wouldn't have flexed Imagination's muscles so early. If my aunt, Sr. Maire du Rosaire, had not introduced me to C.S. Lewis, I would not have believed. If I had not been introduced to the folklore of Kingfishers by my Aunts I would never have flown. Thank You.

All writers need supporters. My especial thanks to North West Words and the team-Eamonn Bonnar, Annemarie, Nick, Guy and Deirdre. Judging NWW International Children's Writing Competition was a joy and a privilege. Some of our winners will be the writers of tomorrow. I wish them luck. The unwavering support of Over the Edge Literary Events as steered by Kevin Higgins and Susan Millar Du Mars helped me steer choppy seas. I am grateful.

Thank You, Austin Macauley Publishers for publishing this book, and especially to Saffron Forde for believing in my words. You have all been a pleasure to work with. An especial shout out to Matthew in Finance and to the fabulous Amelia Woods. Jimmy, Rose, Sue, Philippa et al in our London Book Club, Kathleen and Martin, Joanne and Paul and all of my darling cats, most especially Star. For all my forever family and friends: Anne, Donal R., Dáirín and Mark, Mary and Laurie, Caroline and Dawn, Valerie, Oisin, Lorna, Brid, Dave, Chloe, Leo, Ailbhe, James and Livinia, Liz and Trevor, Ken and Carol, Paddy and Sarah, The good ladies of Letter Kenny Active Retirement Club, and Poetry New Hampshire. I am forever grateful you are all in my life.

And finally, for all that is anomalous, long may you be.